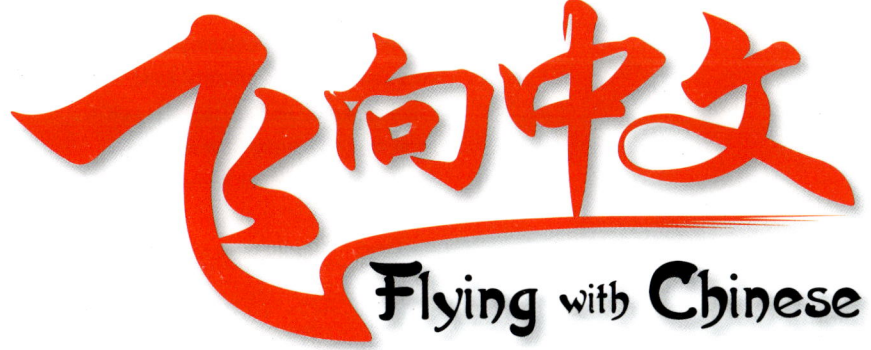

飞向中文
Flying with Chinese

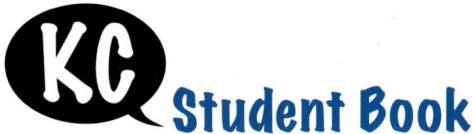

KC Student Book

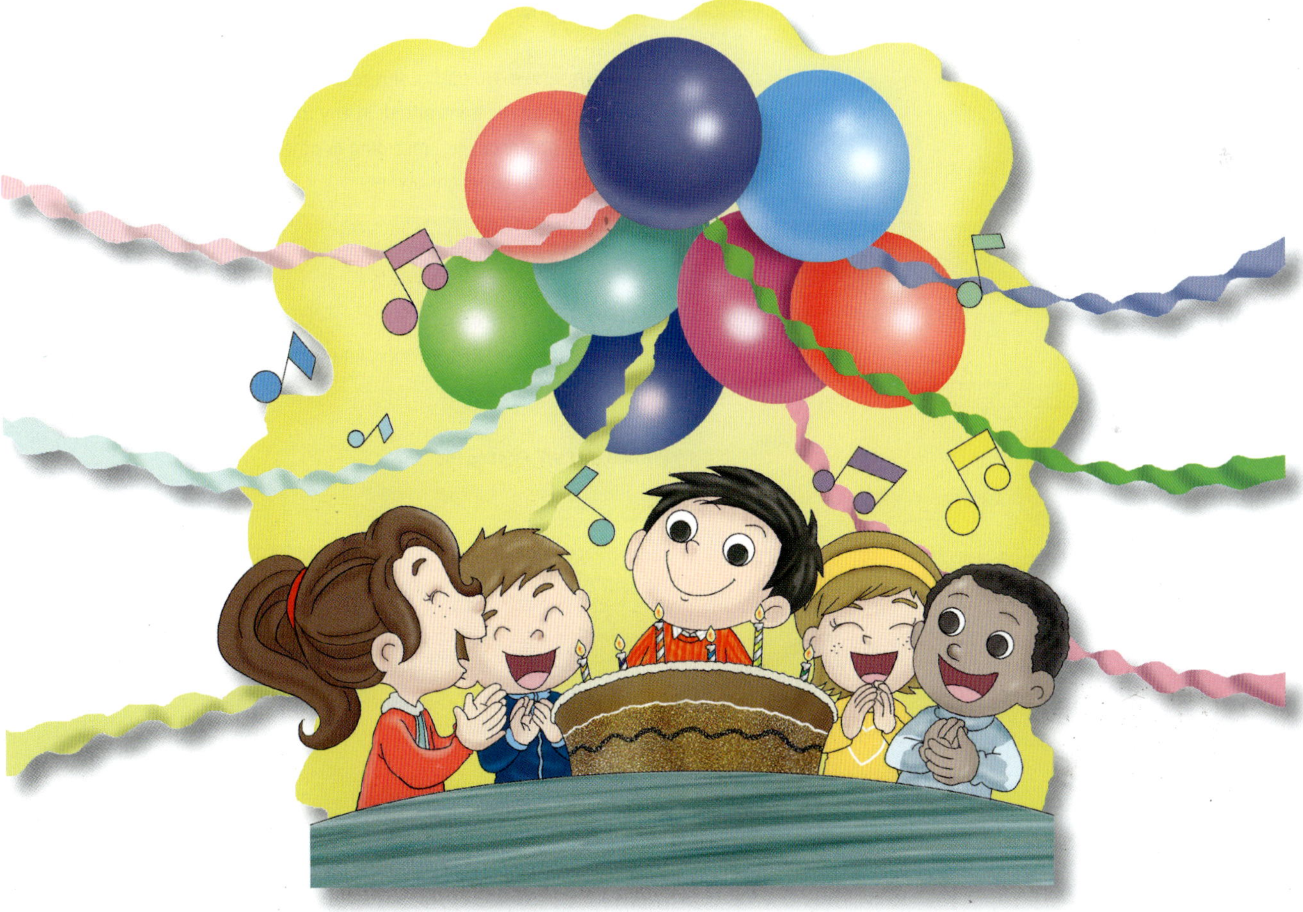

Shuhan C. Wang, Ph. D. • Carol Ann Dahlberg, Ph. D.
Chiachyi Chiu, M.A. • Marisa Fang, M.S. • Mei-Ju Hwang, Ed.D.

Marshall Cavendish Education

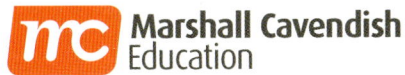

© 2007 Marshall Cavendish International (Singapore) Private Limited

Published by Marshall Cavendish Education
A member of Times Publishing Limited
Times Centre, 1 New Industrial Road, Singapore 536196
Customer Service Hotline: (65) 6411 0820
E-mail: fps@sg.marshallcavendish.com
Website: www.marshallcavendish.com/education/sg

Distributed in North America by:

CHENG & TSUI COMPANY
Bringing Asia to the World™

Cheng & Tsui Company,
25 West St, Boston, MA 02111
www.cheng-tsui.com
Toll Free 1-800-554-1963

First published 2007

All rights reserved. No part of this publication may be reproduced, stored in a retrieval system or transmitted, in any form or by any means, electronic, mechanical, photocopying, recording or otherwise, without the prior permission of the copyright owner.

ISBN 978-981-01-6677-9

Publisher: Lim Geok Leng
Editors: Yvonne Lee   Richard Soh   Rita Teng   Jo Chiu   Chong Liping
Chief Designer: Roy Foo

Printed by KWF Printing Pte Ltd

Preface

Flying with Chinese is a series designed to make the most of children's natural ability to learn language by creating meaningful contexts for learning and guiding them towards language proficiency, literacy development and cultural appreciation. Each book is based on a theme and integrated with other subject areas in the elementary school curriculum.

Flying with Chinese is standards-based and focuses on learners' performance. Some of the important elements in this series include the following:
1. Thematic planning and instruction, with emphasis on the principles and structure of a good story;
2. "Standards for Chinese Language Learning," which is part of the *Standards for Foreign Language Learning in the 21st Century*;
3. Principles of *Understanding by Design*;
4. Matching languages with children (*Languages and Children: Making the Match*).

Under three umbrella themes, each book in the series takes on a different but related sub-theme. These themes are interesting to the learners, connect with the curriculum of the elementary school, promote understanding of Chinese culture, and provide a context for language use.

The Student Book provides the basic story for the lessons, while the Workbook gives learners the opportunity to practice the language and use the concepts presented in the Student Book. The Teacher Guide suggests activities for each day and indicates when the Workbook pages are to be used.

Flying with Chinese focuses on a group of children who are learning Chinese together. These children and their families come from a wide range of backgrounds, and several are heritage Chinese speakers. One member of the group goes to China with her family, where she attends a Chinese school and shares her experiences with her former classmates. Throughout the series learners are introduced to legends, real and fictional characters of importance to Chinese culture, and significant customs, celebrations, and other elements of the Chinese way of life.

Flying with Chinese can be used independently or as part of a sequence of study in a program. Just as a child can fly a kite on his own or in a group, we hope that children will have fun flying these Chinese kites while gaining insight into the Chinese-speaking world.

我的生日会
My Birthday Party

目录 Contents

Lesson 1	我的生日快到了！ My Birthday Is Coming Soon!	1
Lesson 2	你要请谁？ Who Do You Want To Invite?	8
Lesson 3	今天是我的生日 It's My Birthday Today	14
Lesson 4	我们在外面玩 We Play Outside	19
Lesson 5	我们是小小艺术家 We Are Little Artists	27
Lesson 6	寿面和鸡蛋 Longevity Noodles and Chicken Eggs	32
Lesson 7	生日蛋糕 Birthday Cake	38
Lesson 8	爸妈送我生日礼物 Daddy and Mommy Give Me Birthday Presents	45
Lesson 9	朋友送我生日礼物 My Friends Give Me Birthday Presents	53
Lesson 10	我做感谢卡 I Make Thank-You Cards	60
Lesson 11	大家一起来！（评估） I Can Do This! (Performance Assessment Tasks)	66

第1课　我的生日快到了！

一月

二月

三月

四月

我会读　一

五月

		1	2	3	4	5
6	7	8	9	10	11	12
13	14	15	16	17	18	19
20	21	22	23	24	25	26
27	28	29	30	31		

六月

					1	2
3	4	5	6	7	8	9
10	11	12	13	14	15	16
17	18	19	20	21	22	23
24	25	26	27	28	29	30

七月

1	2	3	4	5	6	7
8	9	10	11	12	13	14
15	16	17	18	19	20	21
22	23	24	25	26	27	28
29	30	31				

八月

			1	2	3	4
5	6	7	8	9	10	11
12	13	14	15	16	17	18
19	20	21	22	23	24	25
26	27	28	29	30	31	

我会读　六

我会读 九

我会念

月份歌

一月、二月、

三四月，

五月、六月、

七八月，

九月、十月、

十一十二月。

我会读 生

I can do these things in Chinese, can you?

I can...

- name the months of the year
- tell which month my birthday is
- recite the rhyme "月份歌" with the class
- recognize the *hanzi* "生" and "日", know what they mean and how to say them

第2课 你要请谁?

我会读 请

我会读 要

一　一　一　一

二　二　二　二

I can do these things in Chinese, can you?

I can...

* ask a question about who to invite to a party （你要请谁来？）
* say I have many friends （我有）
* name the friends I want to invite to a party
* sing the song "十个小朋友" with the class
* recognize the *hanzi* "一" and "二", know what they mean and how to say them

小朋友们来我家玩。

我会读 家

我会认

I can do these things in Chinese, can you?

I can...

❖ point out my birthday on the calendar

❖ greet friends and adults when they come to my house（欢迎，请进，……好）

❖ greet friends and adults（老师好，叔叔好，你好）

❖ recognize the *hanzi* "三" and "四", know what they mean and how to say them

第4课 我们在外面玩

我们在外面玩。

我会读 面

我们吹气球。大永吹了一个大气球。

我会读 气

我们玩大风吹。

我会读 风

X X X 五

I can do these things in Chinese, can you?

I can...

❖ tell about playing outside

❖ name two games I like to play

❖ tell if something is big or small

❖ sing and act out the song "我的朋友在哪里？" with the class

❖ recognize the hanzi "五", know what it means and how to say it

第5课 我们是小小艺术家

玩累了，我们进到屋子里面。

我会读 累

玛丽做了一只猫。

荷西做了一只鸟。

我会读　猫

我们玩得很高兴。
我们都是小小艺术家！

我会读　艺

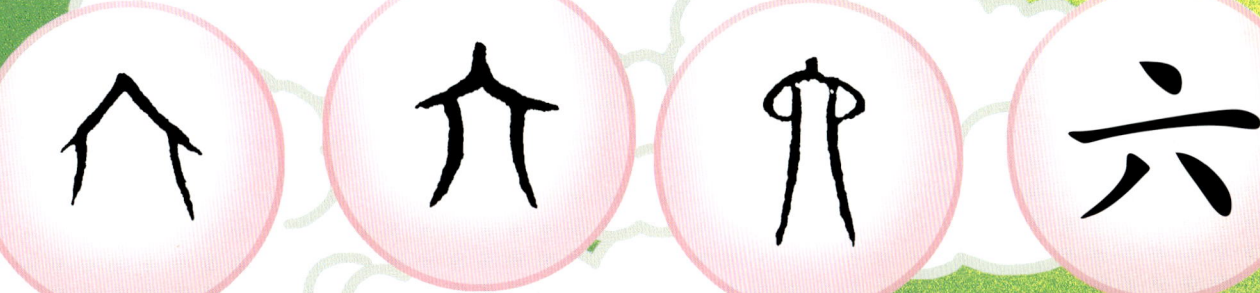

I can do these things in Chinese, can you?

I can...

❖ tell that I'm tired（玩累了）

❖ tell how I feel（玩得很高兴，我们是小小艺术家）

❖ name and make animal shapes with tangrams

❖ recognize the *hanzi* "六", know what it means and how to say it

寿面和鸡蛋

大家肚子饿了。

妈妈给我们吃寿面和鸡蛋。

我会读 面

寿面和鸡蛋又香又好吃。

我会读 蛋

寿面长长的，吃了活到老。

我会读　长

鸡蛋有营养，吃了身体好。

我会读　营

我们吃得很开心！

我会读　开

我会认

七 七 七 七

I can do these things in Chinese, can you?

I can...
- tell someone I am or we are hungry
- name the food most Chinese people eat for birthdays and tell what these food mean
- tell that food tastes or smells good
- recognize the *hanzi* "七", kown what it means and how to say it

第7课 生日蛋糕

妈妈端出一个生日蛋糕。

我会读：糕

蛋糕上面有六支蜡烛。

我六岁了。

我会读　蜡

我们一起唱生日快乐歌。

我会读　起

我会唱

生日快乐歌

祝你 生 日 快 乐

祝你 生 日 快 乐

祝你 生 日 快 乐

祝你 生 日 快 乐

我许了一个心愿。

生日快乐

我吹蜡烛。

我会读　心

妈妈切蛋糕给大家吃。

我会读 切

我会认

八 八 八 八 八

I can do these things in Chinese, can you?

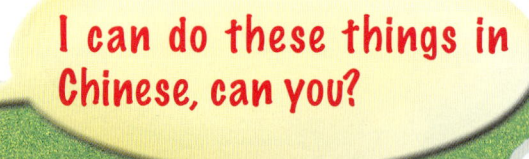

I can...

❖ tell my age
❖ tell about the ways of celebrating birthdays
❖ sing the birthday song "生日快乐" with the class
❖ recognize the *hanzi* "八", know what it means and how to say it

第8课 爸妈送我生日礼物

吃完蛋糕,我拆礼物。

我会读:拆

爸爸送我一个算盘。

我会读　算

爸爸教我们用算盘数数儿。

1 2 3 4 5

＋ －

我会读　盘

妈妈送我一支小笛子。

我会读　笛

妈妈教我吹笛子，呜，呜，呜。

我会读 呜

我谢谢爸爸和妈妈。

我会读 谢

我会念

算盘和笛子

算盘，算盘，会数数，

一二三四五六七。

笛子，笛子，会唱歌，

唱起歌来呜呜呜。

我会认

飞 飞 九 九

I can do these things in Chinese, can you?

I can...
- tell about things related to a birthday party
- tell what gifts Wang Dayong received from his parents
- use an abacus to count numbers
- recite the rhyme "算盘和笛子" with the class
- recognize the hanzi "九", know what it means and how to say it

第9课 朋友送我生日礼物

朋友们送我很多生日礼物。

我会读 送

麦克送我一只玩具小猴子。

我会读 猴

玛丽送我一只玩具熊猫。

我会读 具

莉莉送我一只纸做的鸟。

我会读　纸

我喜欢我的生日礼物。

我会读 礼

我谢谢我的朋友。他们要走了,我向他们说再见。

我会读 走

我会认

丨 亅 十 十

I can do these things in Chinese, can you?

I can...

- name the presents I received for my birthday
- thank people when they give me presents（谢谢）
- tell people I like my presents
- tell that I enjoy doing something
- recognize the *hanzi* "十", know what it means and how to say it

第10课 我做感谢卡

妈妈教我做感谢卡给朋友们。

我会读：感

我要谢谢朋友们来参加我的生日会。

我会读　参

我也做感谢卡给爸爸和妈妈。

我会读　给

我要谢谢爸爸和妈妈送我生日礼物。

我会读 物

过完了生日,我大了一岁。
我是个大孩子了。

我会读 完

我会认

ᗡ ᗡ ᗡ ᕮ 月

I can do these things in Chinese, can you?

I can...
- ❖ tell that I am one year older after my birthday
  （我大了一岁，我是个大孩子了）
- ❖ make a birthday or thank-you card
- ❖ recognize the *hanzi* "月", know what it means and how to say it

第11课 大家一起来!

67

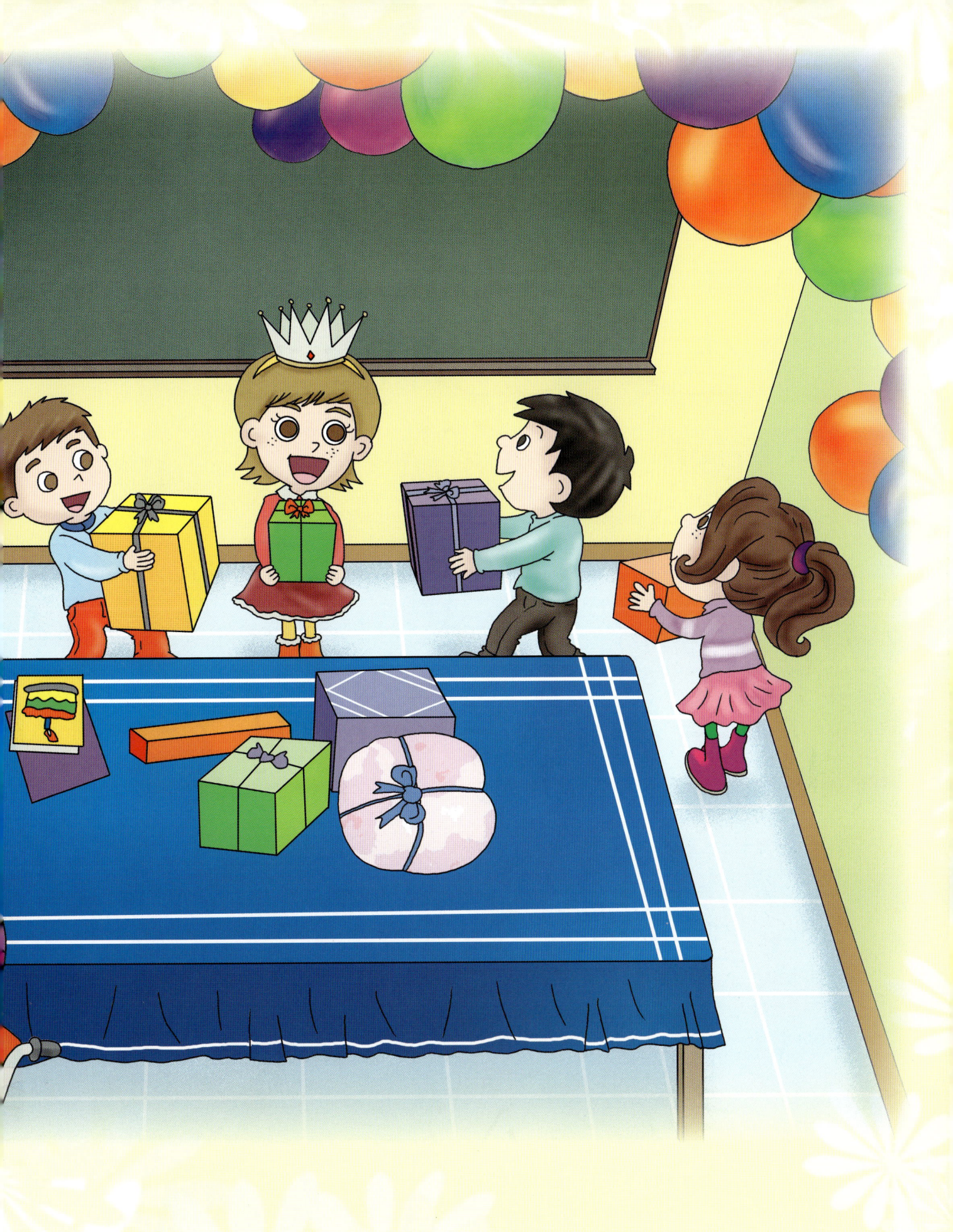

汉字表 Hanzi List

生	四	九
日	五	十
一	六	月
二	七	
三	八	

词汇表 Vocabulary List

Hanzi	Pinyin	English	Page
Lesson 1			
一月	yī yuè	January	1
二月	èr yuè	February	1
三月	sān yuè	March	1
四月	sì yuè	April	1
五月	wǔ yuè	May	2
六月	liù yuè	June	2
七月	qī yuè	July	2
八月	bā yuè	August	2
九月	jiǔ yuè	September	3
十月	shí yuè	October	3
十一月	shí yī yuè	November	3
十二月	shí èr yuè	December	3
我的	wǒ de	my / mine	5

69

Hanzi	Pinyin	English	Page
生日	shēng rì	birthday	5
在	zài	in / at	5
快到了	kuài dào le	almost there	6

Lesson 2

Hanzi	Pinyin	English	Page
你	nǐ	you	8
要	yào	want	8
请	qǐng	to invite	8
谁	shéi	who	8
来	lái	to come	8
生日会	shēng rì huì	birthday party	8
还有	hái yǒu	still have	10
很多	hěn duō	many	10
朋友	péng you	friend	10
可以	kě yǐ	able to	10
十	shí	ten	10
个	gè	(a word of measurement)	10
家里	jiā li	at home	10

Hanzi	Pinyin	English	Page
吗	ma	(final interrogative particle)	10
当然可以	dāng rán kě yǐ	certainly	10
妈妈	mā ma	mother	12
您	nín	you (form of respect)	12
帮	bāng	to help	12
写	xiě	to write	12
邀请卡	yāo qǐng kǎ	invitation card	12

Lesson 3

Hanzi	Pinyin	English	Page
今天	jīn tiān	today	14
是	shì	am / is / are	14
小朋友们	xiǎo péng you men	little friends	15
我家	wǒ jiā	my home	15
玩	wán	to play	15
欢迎	huān yíng	welcome	16
请进	qǐng jìn	Please come in	16
叔叔好	shū shu hǎo	Hello Uncle!	17

Hanzi	Pinyin	English	Page
阿姨好	ā yí hǎo	Hello Auntie!	17

Lesson 4

我们	wǒ men	we	19
外面	wài miàn	outside a particular place	19
吹	chuī	to blow	20
气球	qì qiú	balloon	20
大	dà	big	20
泡泡	pào pao	bubbles	21
小	xiǎo	small	21
大风吹	dà fēng chuī	Big Wind Blows (a Chinese game)	22
捉迷藏	zhuō mí cáng	Hide and Seek	23
玩得好高兴	wán de hǎo gāo xìng	have so much fun	24

Hanzi	Pinyin	English	Page
Lesson 5			
累了	lèi le	tired	27
进到	jìn dào	to go in	27
屋子	wū zi	house	27
里面	lǐ miàn	inside	27
七巧板	qī qiǎo bǎn	Tangrams	28
做了	zuò le	made	28
一只	yì zhī	one (animal), 只 is a word of measurement	28
狗	gǒu	dog	28
猫	māo	cat	29
鸟	niǎo	bird	29
都是	dōu shì	all are	30
小小艺术家	xiǎo xiǎo yì shù jiā	little artist	30

Hanzi	Pinyin	English	Page
Lesson 6			
大家	dà jiā	everyone	32
肚子	dù zi	stomach	32
饿了	è le	hungry	32
给	gěi	to give	32
吃	chī	to eat	32
寿面	shòu miàn	Longevity noodles	32
鸡蛋	jī dàn	chicken eggs	32
又	yòu	and	33
香	xiāng	smell good	33
好吃	hǎo chī	taste good	33
长长的	cháng cháng de	very long	34
活到老	huó dào lǎo	live till an old age	34
有营养	yǒu yíng yǎng	nutritious	35
身体好	shēn tǐ hǎo	healthy	35

Hanzi	Pinyin	English	Page
Lesson 7			
端出	duān chū	to bring out / serve	38
一个	yí gè	one	38
蛋糕	dàn gāo	cake	38
上面	shàng miàn	on top of	39
有	yǒu	have	39
六支蜡烛	liù zhī là zhú	six candles	39
六岁	liù suì	six years old	39
一起	yì qǐ	together	40
唱	chàng	to sing	40
生日快乐	shēng rì kuài lè	Happy Birthday	40
歌	gē	song	40
许了	xǔ le	made (a wish)	42
心愿	xīn yuàn	wish	42
切	qiē	to cut	43

Hanzi	Pinyin	English	Page
Lesson 8			
吃完	chī wán	finish eating	45
拆礼物	chāi lǐ wù	open the gifts	45
送	sòng	to give	46
算盘	suàn pán	abacus	46
教	jiāo	to teach	47
用	yòng	to use	47
数数	shǔ shù	to count numbers	47
一支	yì zhī	one	48
小笛子	xiǎo dí zi	small flute	48
呜，呜，呜	wū, wū, wū	(a sound made by blowing the flute)	49
谢谢	xiè xie	thank you	50

Hanzi	Pinyin	English	Page
Lesson 9			
朋友们	péng you men	friends	53
生日礼物	shēng rì lǐ wù	birthday gifts	53
玩具	wán jù	toys	54
小猴子	xiǎo hóu zi	monkey	54
熊猫	xióng māo	panda	55
纸做的	zhǐ zuò de	made of paper	56
喜欢	xǐ huan	like	57
他们	tā men	they	58
要走了	yào zǒu le	are leaving	58
向	xiàng	to turn towards / face	58
说再见	shuō zài jiàn	say goodbye	58

Hanzi	Pinyin	English	Page

Lesson 10

感谢卡	gǎn xiè kǎ	Thank-You cards	60
给	gěi	to give	60
我要	wǒ yào	I want to	61
参加	cān jiā	to participate	61
也	yě	also	62
大了一岁	dà le yí suì	older by a year	64
大孩子	dà hái zi	big kid	64

I can...

1. tell the month of my birthday
2. invite someone to my birthday party
3. tell someone that I have many friends
4. greet and welcome people when they come to my house
5. tell someone the games I like to play
6. tell my friends that I like to play with Tangrams
7. use Tangrams to make a shape
8. tell someone that I'm hungry
9. tell someone what Chinese people like to eat for their birthdays
10. use an abacus to count numbers in Chinese
11. talk about birthday gifts
12. tell someone my age
13. make a Thank-You or Birthday card
14. tell someone that I had a very happy birthday party
15. sing some Chinese songs